KERNOW

Gwlas Dyberthys

A LAND APART

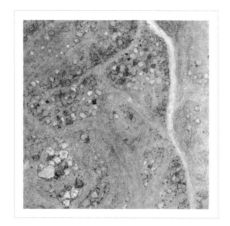

Deborah King

Kemer wyth na wreta gasa an forth coth rag an forth noweth.

Take care you do not leave the old road for the new.

Cornwall stands alone, a 'land apart': it has its own voice, speaks its own language. The rich and varied dialect of the Cornish people reflects a free spirit, an independence born of early Celtic origins. The ancient landscape bares its secrets, shares its history, claiming a powerful and diverse heritage of ecological, archaeological and spiritual significance.

The Duchy's Celtic legacy dates back to the 6th century BC. Although the arrival of Christianity worked to subdue such primitive beliefs, Cornwall remains a strong Celtic nation alongside its western fringe relatives, the Irish, Scots and Manx, holding particularly close links with Welsh and Breton.

The Cornish language exists today in two known forms, Middle and Modern. Circa 1400 AD, English became the official language of Britain and the speaking of Cornish became more and more disadvantageous, the influence of the English pushing further and further west across the Tamar. The last known monoglot speaker of the Cornish language, Dolly Pentreath from Mousehole, died in 1777; it was Henry Jenner who pieced the language back together in the late 19th century, followed by the work of Robert Morton Nance who launched the 'Unified Cornish' system, eventually leading to the formation of the 'Cornish Language Board' in 1967.

Today, it sees a strong revival, the Cornish Gorsedd working to promote both the native tongue and the national Celtic spirit in Cornwall. For the layman, the Cornish word is already accessible in the thousands of Celtic place names. Indeed, Kernow, 'land of the promontory people' is now used as the favoured title for the nation.

Celtic saints also feature prominently, arriving in the 5th-7th centuries from Ireland, Wales and Brittany, to leave a network of churches, stone crosses and holy wells still visited today as places of worship. As with the sacred sites and prehistoric monuments, a unique culture continues to survive here in this western homeland. Maritime endeavour and the enduring spirit of the industrial age have kept alive the ancient folklore and traditions, Arthurian legend living on to preserve an irresistible sense of story, touching the heart and soul of all who come to find this mystical place …

Kernow, gwlas dyberthys.
Cornwall, a land apart.

First edition published in Cornwall, United Kingdom by **wingbeat** publishing limited 2002.
Text and Artwork copyright © Deborah King 2002.
Design © **wingbeat**.
www.wingbeat.co.uk
dk@wingbeat.co.uk

Printed and bound by R. Booth, Penryn, Cornwall.

ISBN   0-9542321-0-0

ACKNOWLEDGEMENTS

My heartfelt thanks to Donald Rawe (*Scryfer Lanwednoc* – Writer of Padstow) for all the care he has taken in the editing of the work; for advice on historical fact and assistance with the Cornish Language. His contribution has proved invaluable to the spirit and serious intention of this book.

My thanks also to Michael Williams (*Gwaryer Lyes-Tu* - Allrounder) for his proof reading and continued support; I would also like to thank Tracey Masterman and the Chase Art Centre, Wadebridge.

I am deeply grateful to my mother, Joy King, for all her enthusiasm and encouragement over the years, and to Teresa Lawton, Helen Cowcher and Chris Andrews for inspiration and exchange of ideas; not forgetting my constant companion, Coscar, for sharing the miles.
Also to all my friends and neighbours in Pencarrow, Advent for their kindness and generosity, most especially Joe and Nikki Driver, who have been closely involved with my progress throughout the two long years of the book's making.

Lastly to my friend and partner in wingbeat, Dave Precious: thank you for believing in me, for sharing the vision and bringing this work so skilfully to the printed page.

Merasta why!

Hallow
ha nansow
dhe'n mor

Moorlands and lowlands to sea

From east to west
to windward
towards land's edge,
I stand on the footings of time:
perfectly aligned with sea and sky,
I heed the silent word of ancient hills,
secrets of the granite
stilled in hallowed space
of this, the first place.

Infinite:
treeless, save the willow carr.
Windswept moors of fescue
peached in shivery swathes
sweep far beneath the ridges and the tors,
topmost stones piled true,
leaning,
resting,
rocking:
Earth's temple,
first monument.

9

Fallen slabs
trip the clitter slopes,
shadows patterning the soil
with fertile pockets:
earth pushing up the sedge
to grip the fragile coil,
the root of darkest age.

Wind the only sound.
Hushed echoes
hum, slow beat on stone.
An ocean breath, salt-laden
stirring voices:
Taw nefra ny on.
Words wake sleeping ground
with maiden tongue,
first language.

Cows nebes ha cows da, mes gwella yu cows nebes.

Speak little and speak good, but speak little is best.

First light
spins and shifts,
lifts from sea on two sides.
Perfect colour
defining *Kernow's* mood:
a restless pride,
a steep and rocky rim.
Here, so close to Earth's core,
closer to the mystery of dawn
I tread softly.
Neolithic fragments
break the skin of primal turf,
history's reminder
should we lose our way,
should we forget the first peoples.

Round houses, rows of handled stone
tumble back to ground.
Barrows, *menhiryon*,
circles in alignment with the sun;
and giant quoits,
high tabled shrines, hold court,
run power of thought across this fabled land.

The old, the spiritual, eclipse my stride.
Holy wells, celtic crosses:
covyon Keltek
carved with care to bless the prayers of saints
stand side by side with chimneys,
quarried heaps and holes.

Progress plays no useful part.

I face the west wind.
I walk lightly towards the day of quiet.
Unhurried, I draw a free breath.
I hear the raven call,
watch the buzzard search for blue in silvered cloud,
sense the drumbeat of distant rain
cold in sunless chill.

My journey skims the peaty streams,
waits by ruddled pool,
reflects its dream.
Clues whisper waves in seas of grass,
wisdom holding counsel in the stone,
backbone of this untouched space.
Kernow's final frontier,
Hallow Bodmeneghy:
the first, the last,
the only place.

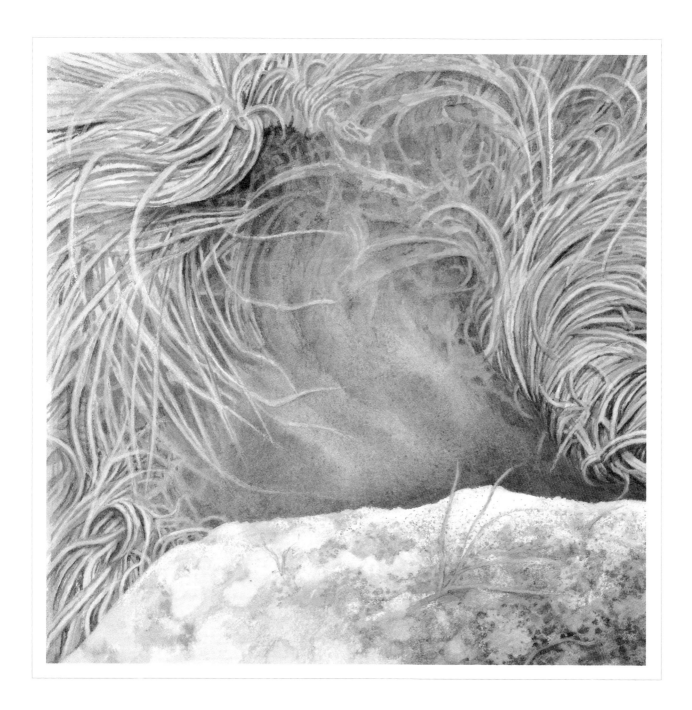

Springs burst the cradle:
transparent link,
a river born
to course the elemental chain,
pure source of rainy hills.
She drinks her fill.

Cool mirrored tide
reflecting every twist and turn.
Chinks of light
quickblink high cloak of oak and ash,
hard shine the shingle
splashed in gold.
The silvered beech
sways guard from guttered floor.

Nothing stirs:

Hedge tightly laid,
folding ground in timbered hush,
last season's harvest crushed,
layer bound in leaf mould,
picture still,
until a fish flicks tail.
A flash of minnow's fin
and then a splash, a lightning dive
winged kingfisher blue,
sapphire bright
burns cool fire.

Flight inspired,
wings beat
then turn in slow repeat.
Sweet spark of memory:
jewel of bedrock
locked in rainwashed, rivered hills,
Alcedo, I see you still…

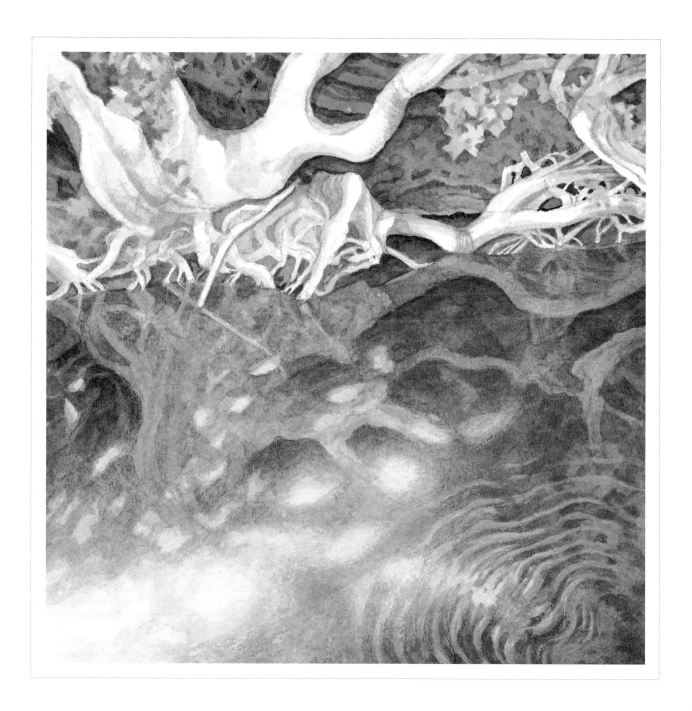

Yn Haf, porth cof Gwaf.

In Summer, remember Winter.

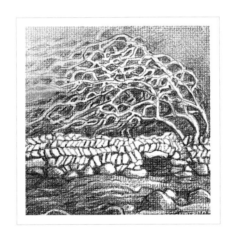

Sharp eye of wind, hard rain,
I turn, avert your gaze.
Await your calm, sun's rays,
sweet pause:
Atlantic holding breath
as balmy, restive moors
hillwrap their marsh
cold, perfect still.

Clouds spin wool-soft rings towards my feet:
reflective edge laps stone,
uncluttered sound
cut loose,
slipshines a lake of finest glass
to greet me where I walk
in waves of wild goose talk.

A buzzard cries
too high for sport of ravens.
Below, sucked tread of sheep on shortening turf:
quiet sky,
quiet earth.

Quiet pool of winter rain,
glinting with the plovers' silvered flight,
golden by sun's fall
it waits for moon.
In shadow light,
lone curlew ascending…
Kepar ha'nylow clewys war dowr cosel.

Old soul,
into the darkening,
so gently singing.

The lake, a ring of whispers.
A lady's hand outstretched;
three times she brandishes the sword
Excalibur,
bejewelled reward
shines deep.
King Arthur's dying wish
sleeps cool
in well of tears.
Moors washed by cloud,
skies weep to shroud his final word.

Nyns yu gun hep lagas, nanyl ke hep scovarn.

There is no down without an eye, nor hedge without an ear.

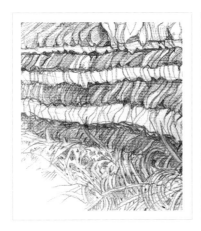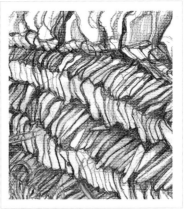

Earth hears my feet
but hilltops hold shy silence.
Bossiney's Mound shades secrets of King Arthur
untouched,
unfound,
laid quiet beneath the blue-chipped, granite ground
steeply tipped to sea.

Curzy-way walls grip the edge
to fall like rivulets of Inny
dripping moss green
down cliff-stacked stone.
One pillar leans
precariously hinged.

Time worn,
cracked,
watching as the ocean turns its back
on bastioned Bossiney,
hill-bottomed,
half-moon haven
for fulmar,
jackdaw,
tumbling raven;

but not for chough,
the blackjack *bran*,
the Cornish daw...

...it talks no more.
No churring, 'chwee-ow' sound.
No wings, no whispered word.

Timebound, touched by tide,
by whims of moon,
Bossiney braves her losses,
defends her truth,
cut with scythe of emerald
bleeding clear Atlantic blue.

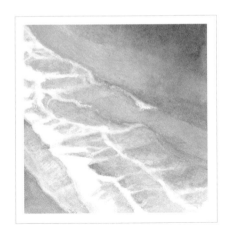

Doves sail the favours of the wind,
chase shadows of *palores*
to take high residence above the castle yard.
A raven guards the iron gate
in wait.
The water falls
darkening a stripe on moss-bright wall.

Tintagel's cliffs curve tall.
Sliced in two by tide to hide a bigger secret.
Sea-hollowed caves
grow wide beneath the castle floor.
Washed by western wave,
jade pools rim stone.
Seals swim the otherworld,
a sorceror's dawn.
When Merlin cradled Arthur to be king
to bring humanity
and hope,
such noble truth was born.

Whath nyns yu marow; ef a vew, hag arta ef a-dhe!

But yet he is not dead; he is alive and he shall come again!

Robert Morton Nance (Mordon)

The mystery unwinds on miller's wall.
Concentric circles spin millenia,
coiled twice
in granite bitten grooves
to turn the labyrinths of chance.

Slow dance of lifetimes in recall
as waters fall to sea on waves of prayer.
Brave knights who kneel,
bow heads to Nechtan.
Kieve's shadows hold your vows,
cast healing powers
of gold: old souls,
pale memory, pure light.
Enduring truth
avails the quest for Holy Grail.

My journey
bends a trail through Rocky Valley's curves.
Emotion flooding stone
to spill Trewethet's Gut
at river's end:
miller's wheel
still turning,
whispering ...
Nyns yu dalleth,
nyns yu deweth:

There is no beginning,
there is no end.

Tek yu hedrogh.

Beautiful is fragile.

Earth's skull dressed soft:
clifftop's crown
cropped in moss and yellow spurge,
such gentle verge…

to quarried vaults, deep cuts
gutted slice by slice from cliff's bone.
Skin deckle-edged, untidy,
heart ribbed in stone,
entombed,
a spine free-standing:
stripped core of Lanterdan,
cliff's muse.

Armorican, this land,
stood brave before the dawn
to fall. As warm seas rise,
fate points its toe,
heel taps the ocean sand.

Dha oryon yu'n ebron, an Damar ha'n mor,
Ha prest yma Arthur ow' quytha dha dhor!

Your boundaries are the sky, the Tamar and the sea,
and still Arthur is guarding your country.

Edmund Henry Hambly (*Gwas Arthur*)

Time folded, faulted strand,
man-handled, drilled in beaded cave,
walls tipped steep.

I walk the fissured ledge
grooved by time's tread,
by lead-capped boots,
tram wheels and hooves.
Waters polish floor a mineral blue,
a smooth metallic tinged with pleats of silver,
skiddy, stripped bare
where pools of cyan
sink cool stare through schist of stone;
slabs pale hour by hour
in sunlight,
scored, stipple-veined,
quartz pink, boned link,
Devonian line ingrained.

Old tracks, new land:
far sweeping strand
of musselled decks snapped shut,
sun-touched,
black-racked buttress for salt washed stone.

The gulls tread floor,
idling between tides
side by side along the shore
in line for what the sea might bring:
already rising,
spilling from its rim,
seeping unseen
wave by wave
to fill pink-lipped pools
a cool aquamarine.

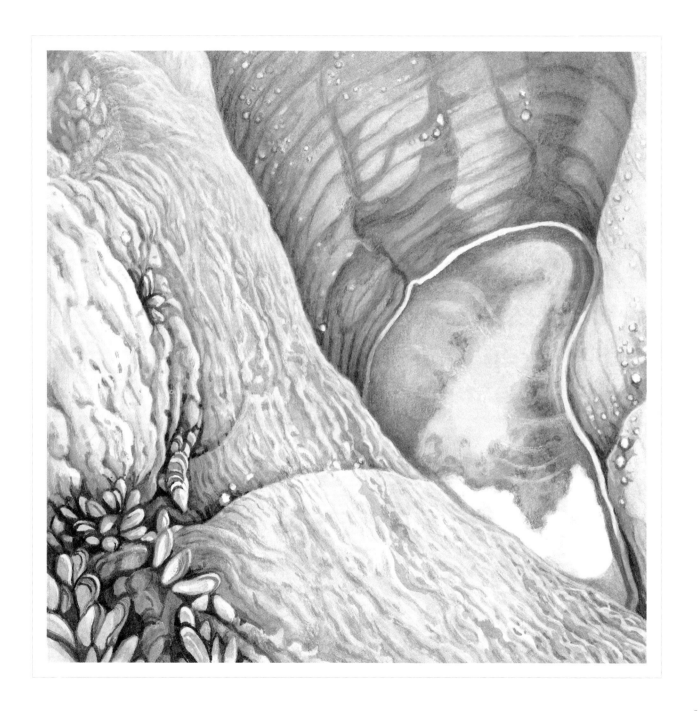

Sands shrink:
dark curves recoil the wavy edge,
the brink of blue.
Barnacles clinch rock.
Tight lock of limpets grip the ledge
as caves resound their final warning.

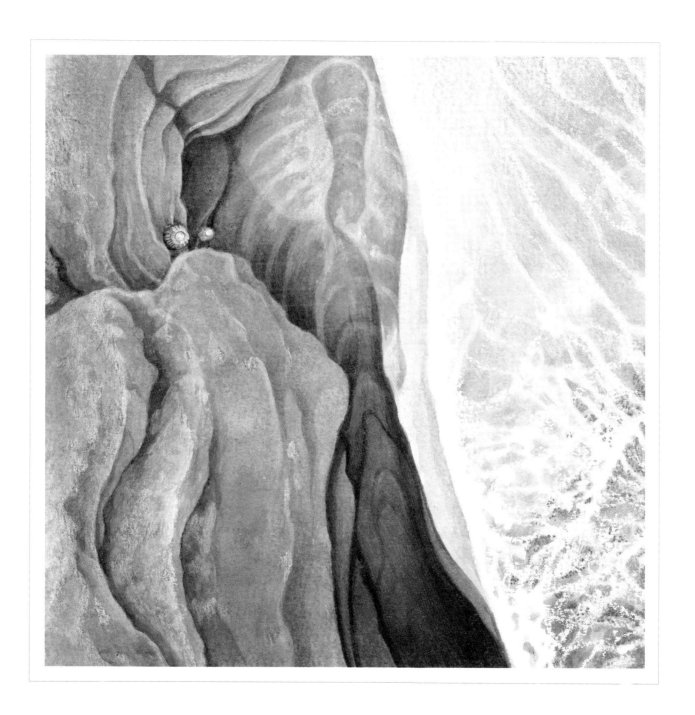

Morlanow nyns yu dal travyth.

The morning tide is not worth nothing.

Penhallic waits,
recalls her ships to shore.
Her wharf casts sylvan shadows,
masts creaking,
speaking still…
Gorhel whath a-wol.

Stone, the silent witness
soaking sun's heat,
channelling earth's fire
to meet tide's roll.

A last dance
as black-backs chance the salted floor.
Gwylanas in mezzotint,
first wave
imprints a mirrored stroll.

Washed clean this rutted land.
Rolled soft by cloud
and cerulean sea,
come to heal Trebarwith's strand
untamed, still proud
despite the careless touch of man's cruel hand.

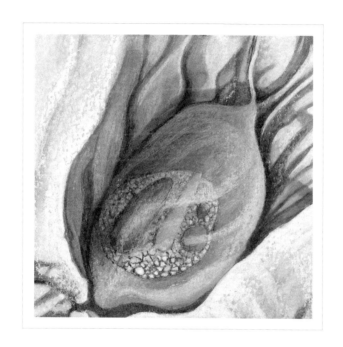

Whath arta lanwes mor a dhe, rag gorhel myghtern lowr.

The flowing of the tide will come again, enough for a king's ship.

Robert Morton Nance (Mordon)

Land's rise and fall,
both cruel and kind,
hems a weathered edge.
Smooth hillock, perfect round
looms proud above Dun Bar,
her cambered brow
curves tight to cloud,
sap spilling from a silk of early green
to stir new sound.

Cows nebes, cows da. Ha da' vyth cowsys arta.

Speak little, speak good. And good will be spoken again.

Soft hum of spring:
first flower,
first tortoiseshell to flap wings
dust the waking hour.
A moment's fan,
a flit of rusted gold in wind's warm shadow.
Upbeat the skylark
wingbeats to heaven,
song's sweet flow to earth
where rings of surf
shine rocks of turquoise, violet, jade
of every tint and shade.
Blue wave, dark line, ebb tide.

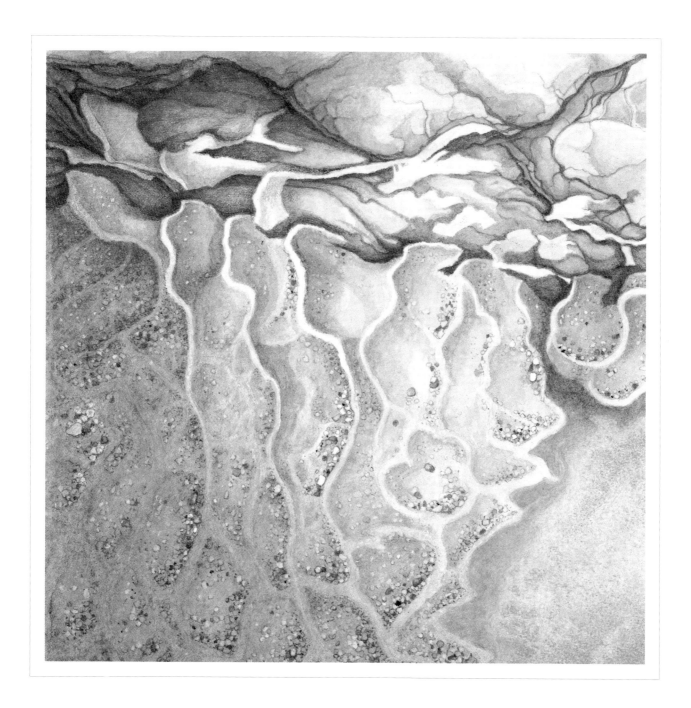

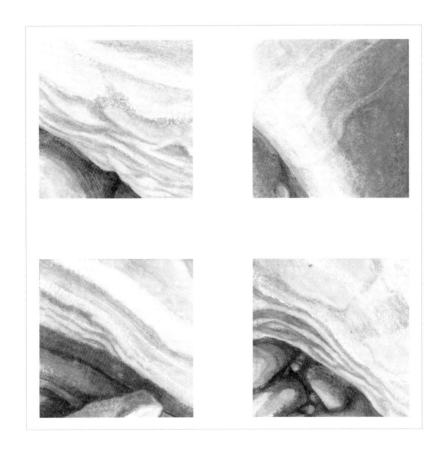

I stay here with St. Enodoc.
And walk the widening mile to river's end,
slate spire leaning for a clearer view
from where the Poet knew, one day
he'd lay his head,
his words
still heard to sing on *Kernow's* ground.

Rag bynytha bys vynary,
the footsteps dance.
Soft rhythm skitters stone:
seafaring souls unlocked,
short lives
three tiers deep
unknown,
unnamed,
unnumbered, sleep to dream
sweet memory.

Sacred foothills,
once haunt of hazel, oak and yew
now forest grave.
High duned,
stone walled by saint's cave
blessed by holy well,
by tune of bells.

O summer wind,
roll Sahel's song to sea.
Toll western lands;
summon us to Sinkinniny church
so we may hear sweet voices
beneath the windblown sand.

Den heb tavas a gollas y dyr.

A man without a language has lost his land.

I hear the seagull cry
but not the chough,
the hermit crow to haunt the cliffs,
spin tricks around the wind.
Red sickle bill, brown eye
black wing,
sing one more song.
Bring word of Arthur,
fly him home to me.

An howl a splannas war an balores,
Hag ena kefys spyrys gwyr Kernow.
The sun shone on the chough
and there I found the true spirit of Cornwall.

Mary Royle (Pendenhar)

I came west.
I took the top road northbound to the edge.
High moors released their grip, tor's shadow
slipped my shoulder, reminding me
of old ground, first footings.

Before me now, a wider view:
Atlantic brow brims blue from ear to ear.
The planet curves the way it should,
the four winds merge
up here. ———

Land stops short.
Cliffs stall in deadlock,
hard standing, steepening crags cleave closure.
Waves cut small difference.

Big skies, big winds.
Clouds mercurial,
rain free to change its mind.
Hills hold their winding lane
down,
down
where Jordan meets Valency,
dark shade, cool descent.

We flow the same way.
'Onen hag Oll'
Boscastle bares her raw, sequestered soul.

Pobel a bell a-bew castylly.

People afar own castles.

Hills may hide your mysteries
but tide's withdrawal lets me tap your vein.
Your chains fall slack,
your wall exposed:
tall boned stack. Black washed,
tight laid in rows of narrowed stone
slabbed upright,
sculpted to a serpent's curve,
tucked pause.

I walk your rutted cob, your cobbled deck.
I hear your blowhole spill its guts,
spew its protest,
the restive hills bewitched,
benign.

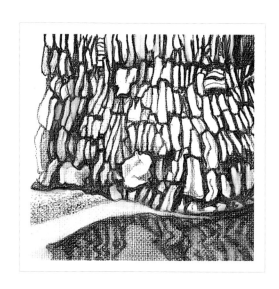

A final glance:
a profile well defined,
keeps silent watch.
Penally, dressed in pink,
so soon persuaded…

One murmur from the ocean and she drinks,
she draws her fill.
Sea swells jacuzzi swirl in trackless deep,
whirlpools of turquoise,
welled coils of perfect green
beneath.

Above,
gulls hang her upfurl
perfect white.
Fulmars glide precision flight,
fate's swingwing shadows flit the lower ledges,
brave the edge

as Land Apart...

awaits the dawning wave.

Oh, shy haven, safe harbour,
your castle in the air holds such lost dreams.
Ghost bells ring your seas off Forrabury.
A ship still sails,
her stories fill the wind:
I think I hear her singing.

Na sconyeugh an Geltyon hag oll aga geryow!
Gwreugh cara ˙gas tavas en termen termennow,
Ha gwedhen an Gernow gwra lesa hy delyow.

Do not refuse the Celts and all their words!
Love your language for ever and ever,
and the tree of Cornwall will spread its leaves.

W.C.D.Watson. (*Tyrvap*)

GLOSSARY

2. **Rocky Valley Carving** detail (see P.41)

5. **Rough Tor** from Fernacre Stone Circle, Bodmin Moor.

7. **Granite Moorland Pool** near Showery Tor.
8. *'rocking'* A reference to the Logan Stone, delicately balanced due to horizontal weathering of the ancient core stones on the peaks of Rough Tor, sacred hilltop site, Bronze Age stone fort and Cornwall's second mountain at 400 metres above sea level.
Pronounced 'Rowter' it derives from the Cornish word *Rowtor* meaning ruler, monarch.

9. **Looking towards Brown Willy** from Little Rough Tor.
Brown Willy derives from *bron wennyly* 'swallows hill'.

10. **Stone Sculpture.** Remains of the heavily folded and faulted Armorican Mts. which stretched down the south west peninsula some 250 million years ago. Molten rock from the earth's interior welled up in the heart of these mountains, then cooled and consolidated under pressure, gradually exposed by erosion to become the granite moorland spine of Cornwall, finally disappearing into the Atlantic beyond the Isles of Scilly.

11. **Moorland Pool** on site of ancient roundhouse.

12. *Taw nefra ny on.* 'We shall never be silent'
13. **Moorland Rockpool** below Rough Tor.

14. **Middle Moor Cross** near St. Breward. A wheel-headed wayside cross standing beside an ancient track running towards Roughtor. There is a tradition that whenever this cross hears the bells of *Semmenward* (St. Breward) it spins around and falls down.
16. *menhiryon* 'Longstones' i.e. Standing Stones.
A **round house** settlement may consist of up to a hundred dwellings, as seen on and around Bodmin Moor where many Bronze Age villages survive, spread over vast distances in field systems complete with tracks and droveways. Fine examples can be found close to Rough Tor. **Barrows** can also be found on the moors, the bowl-shaped barrow or stone cairn most often seen. An excellent example of a ring cairn stands on Showery Tor, north of Rough Tor. A triple bell barrow, one of only three in Britain, exists close to the moors in Advent.

Standing stones, menhirs. A few survive in this moorland region, usually in alignment with cairns and sacred sites, the tallest of which stands at Moorgate measuring nine feet.

Stone circles. Bodmin Moor has fine examples of these ancient ceremonial sites, including Fernacre circle of 52 visible stones and Stannon circle with 81 visible stones. Multiple circles also occur. A pair stand on King Arthur's Downs and a line of three circles, The Hurlers, survive at Minions. Nine Stones at Alternun form the smallest circle.

Quoits, or chamber tombs are among the earliest of all the surviving monuments. Fine examples of these are Pawton Quoit near Wadebridge and Trethevy Quoit near St. Cleer.

Inscribed stones date from the late Iron Age and Dark Age period when Cornwall developed strong links with Ireland, Wales and Brittany. Kernow was then part of the kingdom of Dumnonia and many of the stones use both Latin and Celtic lettering in memorial to their leaders.

The Slaughter Bridge Stone, believed to commemorate the site of King Arthur's last battle, lies by the river near Camelford, a town claiming close links with Camelot and the Arthurian Legend. King Doniert's Stone near St. Cleer stands in two pieces, fine examples of decorative carving commemorating Cornish King Dungarth who drowned, possibly in the River Fowey.

Holy wells and Celtic crosses mostly date from the Dark Ages, the stone crosses standing as holy markers and preaching stones, some erected in honour of the holy men and women, the Celtic saints who travelled from Ireland, Wales and Brittany.

Although Christianity was gaining influence, the customs and beliefs of the people maintained strong links with the megalithic monuments of their ancestors. Fine examples of sacred wells still exist in the villages of St. Cleer and St. Clether close to Bodmin Moor.

'covyon Keltec' 'Celtic memories'

'chimneys, quarried heaps and holes' refers to Cornwall's industrial past. Most of the mining and quarrying excavation on and around the moors concentrated on slate, granite and china clay, although ventures were also made for copper, tin, manganese, antimony, lead and silver.

17. **The Slaughter Bridge Stone** near Camelford.
18. *Hallow Bodmeneghy* 'Moors of Bodmin'
Bodmeneghy translates as 'monk's dwelling'. In medieval times Bodmin was the religious centre for all Cornwall.

19. **Moorland Pool.** Stannon.
20. *'Springs burst...'* A reference to the rise of the River Camel on Bodmin Moor.
'Camel' derives from the Cornish word *cam* meaning crooked or curved, *heyle* meaning estuary. Beyond the town of Camelford, the river is joined by numerous moorland streams forging their way through narrow valleys, gorges and medieval woodlands towards the sea.

21. **Camel Valley.** Pencarrow, Advent.

22. *Alcedo* Old Cornish name for kingfisher. (R. Morton Nance. see bibliography)
23. **Kenningstock** near Tressiney, Advent.

24. **A Cornish Hedge** including 'sheeps creep', a tunnel feature allowing the smaller stock freedom of movement. Such hedges are pre-13th century, many moorland walls dating from pre-history forming the boundaries to field systems still existing after 3000 years.

25. **Winter Trees.** Advent.

27. **Crowdy Lake.** Davidstow Moor.
Once marshland, now reservoir and wildfowl refuge close to Rough Tor. Situated high on the moor close to marsh habitat, the site is also important for invertebrates.

28. *keper ha'n ylow clewys war dowr cosel.* 'like the music heard on still waters'

29. 'A lady's hand' Many legends surround the natural moorland pool of Dozmary, but its most famous association is its link with the passing of Arthur.
As the King lay mortally wounded after the Battle of Camlann, he instructed Sir Bedivere to return Excalibur to the Lady of the Lake. With some reluctance, Bedivere finally granted his dying wish. As the mighty sword was thrown to the waters, it was received by an outstretched hand, shaken three times before disappearing forever into the deep.

30. **Cornish Hedge.** These granite boundaries appear in various different shapes and styles. The older walls are often sinuous in shape, built to follow the course of natural features such as streams and ploughed furrows. This is a 'curzyway' wall, common in North Cornwall and built in herringbone style.
'Bossiney's Mound' Presumably a Bronze Age site believed to conceal Arthur's Round Table. On midsummer night it is supposed to rise in a flash of light, illuminating the sky for a moment before sinking back to the earth.

31. **Elephant Rock.** Bossiney.
'Inny' A reference to the River Inny rising on Davidstow Moor.

32. Bossiney. Translates to mean 'Cyni's dwelling'. Village bordering Tintagel.
bran Cornish word for crow.
'Cornish Daw' Traditional Cornish name for the chough, once so prolific in the county, it was referred to as the Cornish Chough across the UK. Considered to be the most charismatic of all the crows, it is affectionately known by many names in Cornwall including, Cornish Jack, Cornish Kae, Hermit Crow and Palores. The last wild choughs nested here in 1952. So revered is the chough, it takes pride of place on the crest of Cornwall's Coat of Arms, its red claw grasping the Ducal crown.

33.  **Coast path**. Benoath, Bossiney.

34. **Atlantic Blue**. Bossiney.
36. *palores.* A Cornish name for chough meaning 'digger'.
‘castle yard’ A reference to the inner courtyard of Tintagel Castle. The land bridge connecting the ‘Island’ to the mainland once carried the defences of an Iron Age cliff castle before its erosion and eventual collapse *c.*1300 AD. On the landward side, remains of a Dark Age settlement still survive, possibly the seat of the High Kings of Dumnonia between the 5th and 7th centuries AD.

‘iron gate’ A defended wharf where goods were brought ashore.

37. **Low Tide.** Merlin’s Cave, Tintagel.
38. ‘Tintagel’ From *dyn tagell* meaning ‘fort of the narrow neck’.
The link between Arthur and Tintagel was first suggested by Geoffrey of Monmouth in his ‘History of the Kings of Britain’. Here grew the powerful folk-belief that Arthur was not dead, but would come again and return to his birthplace. (see P.39)
‘Merlin cradled Arthur’ Arthur’s story is said to begin in the fortress of Tintagel.
Aided by the magical powers of the sorceror, Merlin, Arthur was born and entrusted to his care, claiming the throne at the age of fifteen. It was Merlin who devised the ‘Sword in the Stone’ test to confirm that Arthur was the rightful king, ruling over 30 kingdoms. As Arthur’s magician and counsellor, Merlin helped to acquire Excalibur from the Lady of the Lake, supposedly from Dozmary Pool on Bodmin Moor (see P.29). He also made the Round Table, which became Arthur’s on his marriage to Guinevere, who as he predicted, was to bring about the downfall of the King through her affair with Lancelot. This led to the Battle of Camlann, reputedly at Slaughterbridge, Camelford (see P.17).

39. **Tintagel Castle**. The remaining battlement wall of the courtyard.
‘Whath nyns yu marrow;’ From ‘He shall come again’ a poem by Robert Morton Nance.
(Mordon – sea wave) 1873-1959. Artist and maritime historian (see P.3).
40. ‘miller’s wall’ Ruined mill Rocky Valley, Tintagel, displaying two maze-like carvings (see P.41). Similar to Galician designs found throughout Britain, Ireland and the Atlantic seaboard of Europe, considered to be Bronze Age, but possibly carved by the miller in more recent times.
‘Kieve’s shadows’ A reference to St. Nectan’s Kieve, situated in the wooded valley of St. Nectan’s Glen, near Tintagel. At the head of the Glen is a waterfall, which has associations with the Celtic water-god Nechtan later christianised to become St. Nectan. The waterfall is now designated (SSSI) as one of ten most spiritual sites in the country. The Kieve is a potent symbol of Mother Earth and has been a place of worship and healing since pre-Christian times. Legend has it that it was once visited by the Knights of the Round Table prior to their search for the Holy Grail.

41. **Rocky Valley Carving**. Near Trethevy, Tintagel.
'Trewethet's Gut' Steep gorge and outlet where the sacred valley waters meet the sea.

43. **Rockpool.** Bossiney.
44. 'quarried vaults' Virtually the entire coastal edge from Tintagel to Trebarwith has been utterly transformed by the quarrying of slate. During the last 500 years, ten quarries have worked the cliffs and the remains of splitting sheds and tramways can still be seen from the coast path.
The rock in North Cornwall is known as Upper Devonian. It is composed of sheets of Devonian and Carboniferous sedimentary and volcanic rocks, originally deposited some distance apart, to be slid into their present position and layered on top of each other in intense folding and faulting cliff structures. Igneous activity during this period was to form the highly compressed and easily cleaved slates of today, still quarried and cut by hand nearby at Delabole.
'Lanterdan' 80 foot tall pinnacle rising from the quarry floor in Lanterdan Quarry, between Trebarwith and Bagalow.
'Armorican' A reference to the Armorican Mountains which stretched down the south-west peninsula some 250 million years ago (see No.10).

45. **Cliff Face** (details) Lanterdan Quarry.
'Dha oryon yu'n ebron....' A line from the poem 'God be with you Cornwall'
by Edmund Henry Hambly (*Gwas Arthur* – Servant of Arthur) 189* – 197*.
46. 'mineral blue' As well as the occasional thin layers of limestone, the slate also takes on a pale greyish-green hue, weathering to a pale silvery-grey, due to the green mineral chlorite known as 'greenschist'. Other volatile substances were to rise through the granite, squeezing out through weakening lines and cracks, gradually cooling to form mineral veins. The most common of these is quartz, also found in larger crystal pieces along this part of the coast.
'Devonian' (see No. 44)

47. **Rockpool.** Trebarwith.

48.  **Hole Beach.** Trebarwith.
49. as above (detail)

51. **Pink-lipped Pool.** Benoath Cove.

52.  **Rock Strata.** Trebarwith.
53. **Limpets.** Trebarwith.

54.  **Ledges.** Low tide, Trebarwith.
55. as above (detail)

56. 'Penhallic' A reference to Penhallic Point (between Trebarwith and Tintagel) where a zig-zag donkey track can still be seen descending the cliffs to a wharf from where sailing ships transported the slate. The cargo was lowered into the hold by a projecting crane standing 100 feet up on the clifftops.
'Gorhel whath a-wol' 'A ship still sails'
'gwylanas' 'gulls'

57. **Rockpool.** Pentireglaze, to the west.

58. **Gull Rock.** Trebarwith Strand.
59. **Rockpool.** Trebarwith.

60.  **Low Tide.** Trebetherick Point. Near Daymer Bay, Camel Estuary.
61. as above (detail)
'The flowing of the tide.' Line from the poem 'King Arthur is not dead!'
by Robert Norton Nance (Mordon) 1873–1959 (see P.3 & No.39).

62. 'Dun' Known now as Doom Bar, a sand bar across the Camel Estuary, responsible for the wrecks of numerous ships seeking shelter from Atlantic storms.
Brea Hill. Roman hill fort. Camel Estuary.
63. **Sand Dunes.** Near Rock, Camel Estuary.
The Camel Estuary is the one major break in the coast of North Cornwall. It is an immensely varied system largely dominated by sand and it is an important refuge for migrating, wintering waders and wildfowl.
65. **Mudflats.** Daymer Bay. Camel Estuary.

66. **Low Tide.** Daymer Bay.
67. These illustrations describe the colour changes found in the rocks around the north side of Daymer Bay, consisting of additional bands of purple and green. These two colours are due to the two different oxidation states of iron. Red, maroon and purple indicates ferric iron and the green and turquoise variations indicate ferrous iron, reflecting the alternating type of sediment washed into the sea from the adjacent continent.

68. 'St. Enodoc' Name given to the church in Trebetherick overlooking Daymer Bay.
'the Poet' refers to the Poet Laureate, Sir John Betjeman (1906-1984) who spent much of his life in Trebetherick. His gravestone stands in the churchyard, just inside the Lych Gate, where his mother is also buried. There is a tablet in memory of his father inside the church.
'*Rag bynytha bys vynary*' 'For ever and ever'
'seafaring souls' A reference to the 'unknown sailors' whose ships were wrecked on Doom Bar while seeking shelter in the Camel Estuary. Some of these ancient graves are three tiers deep.

St. Enodoc Church. Trebetherick.

69.  'forest grave' Refers to the great gale in 1857 when the sand dunes shifted to reveal the remains of a prehistoric forest. The sands have long since covered them again, and almost completely buried the church at times during the 18th/19th centuries, hence the name 'Sinkininny'.
'saint's cave' It is believed that part of the church was built over St. Enodoc's cave. A small spring has been discovered under flagstones beyond the rood screen and St. Enodoc may have made his hermitage close by.
'holy well' A reference to the Jesus Well, half a mile away, where St. Enodoc may have taken his converts to be baptised.
'Sahel' The present bell in the church tower was purchased in 1875 from a ship from Southern Italy, wrecked between Daymer and Polzeath. It bears the inscription 'Sahel' suggesting it once belonged to an older vessel.

70. **Cornish Skies.**
71. 'Bring word of Arthur' In legend, the chough personifies the spirit of Arthur. The bird became protected as a result, the soul of King Arthur fabled to have returned to Cornish shores in the guise of a chough (see No.32).
'*An howl a splannas...*' Quote from the poem 'The Black Bird'
by Mary Royle (*Pendenhar*) Journalist and historian. 1926 -

73. **Rock Ledge** near Polzeath.

75. **Clifftop.** Willapark, Boscastle.
76. 'Jordan meets Valency' Jordan Valley lies close to the access road to Boscastle where it converges with the Valency River and runs down to meet the sea.
'*Onen hag Oll*' 'One and all' as used on the coat of arms of Cornwall.
'Boscastle' Derives its name from Bottreaux Castle, the old baronial residence of the Bottreaux family. The castle has long since vanished. Since before the 16th century, this tortuous harbour operated as a thriving port, vessels towed or 'hobbled' in by rowing boats, aided by horses along the towpath. Its chief exports were slate, minerals and corn.

77.
78.
79.

Boscastle Harbour.
'Tall boned stack' A reference to the medieval breakwater and ancient harbour walls.
Medieval Breakwater. Boscastle.
'final glance' Refers to Profile Rock, so called due to its apparent likeness to Queen Victoria. It is situated close to the famous blow hole.
'Penally' Penally Point, headland on the north side of the harbour exit.

80.
81.
82.

Atlantic Blue. (detail)
Clifftop. Willapark, Boscastle.
'Ghost bells' Although the tower of Forrabury church has stood silent for centuries, there is a legend based on the writings of Rev. Robert Stephen Hawker of Morwenstow that bells ring from beneath the waves to warn of approaching storms. The church overlooks the Forrabury stitches, a system of Celtic land tenure known as 'stitchmeal', one of only three surviving examples still existing in Britain today.

The Forrabury Cross. Wheel-headed wayside cross by the church path. Three holes in the shaft suggest it was once used as a gatepost.

83.
84.

Atlantic Wave.
'Na sconyeugh an Geltyon ...' From the poem 'I hear'
by W.C.D. Watson (*Tyrvap* – Son of the Land.) 188* – 1959.
Watson was one of the founding Bards of the revived Cornish Gorseth and greatly regarded as one of the finest speakers of Cornish this century.

85.

Windswept Tree. North Cornwall.

86.

St. Piran's Flag. St. Piran was the Patron Saint of Cornish Tinners and thus, a Patron of Cornwall. St. Piran's cross stands near Perranporth close to the remains of the historical chapel and oratory, *circa* 7th century. His flag was to become the Cornish banner. The white cross on a black background not only signifies triumph over evil, but more specifically represents molten tin flowing from the black ore. This flag has been adopted as the National Emblem of Cornwall.

SELECT BIBLIOGRAPHY.

BERE, Rennie: Nature of Cornwall. *Barracuda Books in assoc. with the Cornwall Naturalists' Trust.*
BETJEMAN, Sir John: Collected Poems. 1958. *John Murray.*
BRISTOW, Colin M: Cornwall's Geology and Scenery. *Cornish Hillside Publications.*
COOMBS, Franklin: The Crows. A study of the Corvids of Europe. *B.T. Batsford Ltd.*
DAVISON, Brian K: Tintagel Castle. *English Heritage.*
JENNER, Henry: The Celts in Cornwall. 1916. *Oakmagic Publications.*
LANGDON, Andrew: Stone Crosses in N.Cornwall. *First pub. Federation of Old Cornwall Societies.*
NANCE, Robert Morton: Article 'The Celtic Bird-Names of Cornwall'. *Published by Old Cornwall Magazine. '62.*
                                                    Fed. of Old Cornish Societies.

RAWE, Donald R: A Prospect of Cornwall. *Lodenek Press.*
SAUNDERS, Tim (ed.):   The Wheel. Anthology of Modern Poetry in Cornish. 1850-1980. *Francis Boutle Publications.*
STRAFFON, Cheryl: The Earth Mysteries Guide to Bodmin Moor and N.Cornwall. *Meyn Mamvor Publications.*
THOMPSON, E.V: Discovering Bodmin Moor. *Bossiney Books.*
WEATHERHILL, Craig: Cornish Place Names and Language. *Sigma Leisure.*
                             Cornovia, Ancient Sites of Cornwall and Scilly. *Cornwall Books.*
WILLIAMS, Michael: About Boscastle. *Bossiney Books.*

Whevrer yu an mys an moyha fell...
mes Whevrer a len an crunyow rag Mys Merth.